my LiTTLE PONY

JUMBO
Coloring & Activity Book

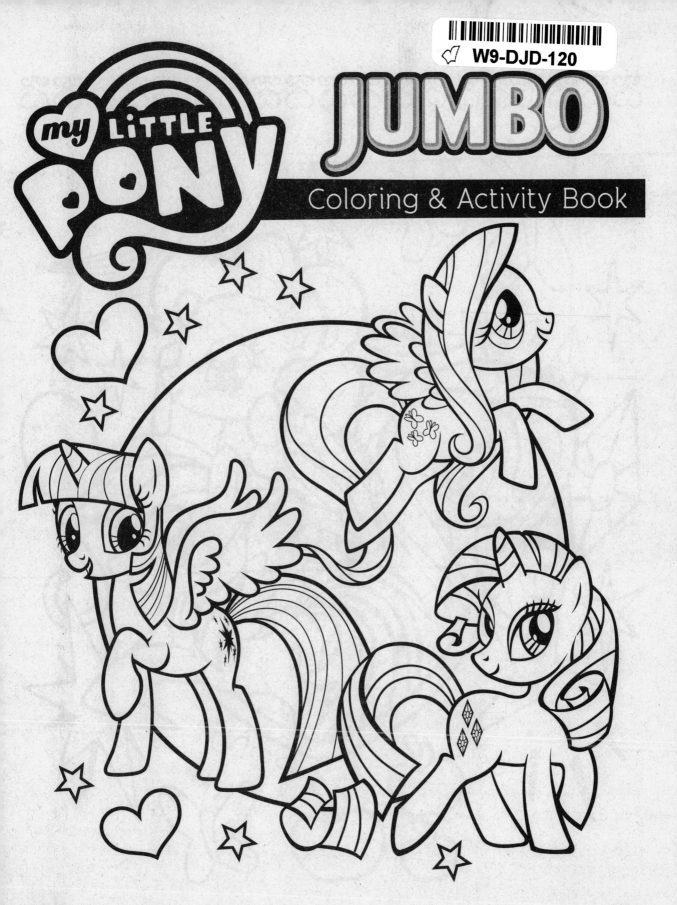

Licensed By:

HASBRO and its logo, MY LITTLE PONY, and all related characters are trademarks of Hasbro and are used with permission. © 2014 Hasbro. All Rights Reserved. Manufactured and distributed by Bendon.

bendon®

The BENDON name, logo and Tear and Share are trademarks of Bendon, Ashland, OH 44805.

WHO IS WHO?

Draw a line from each pony's cutie mark
to her correct name.

①  Ⓐ **FLUTTERSHY**

②  Ⓑ **PRINCESS CELESTIA**

③  Ⓒ **TWILIGHT SPARKLE**

HOW MANY?

Count the items below and place your answer on the line.

_____ APPLES.

CELEBRATE FRIENDSHIP

PONY MAZE

Help Twilight Sparkle find her way
to her favorite books.

finish ◄

start

Rainbow Dash

MY LiTTLE PONY MiX-UP

Unscramble the words below.

AiRNOBW

_____

AFST

_____

LFY

_____

LET'S DRAW!

Use the grid
to help you draw
a flower.

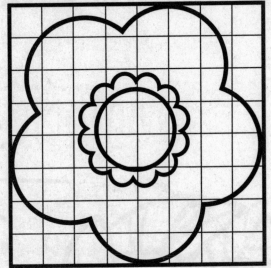

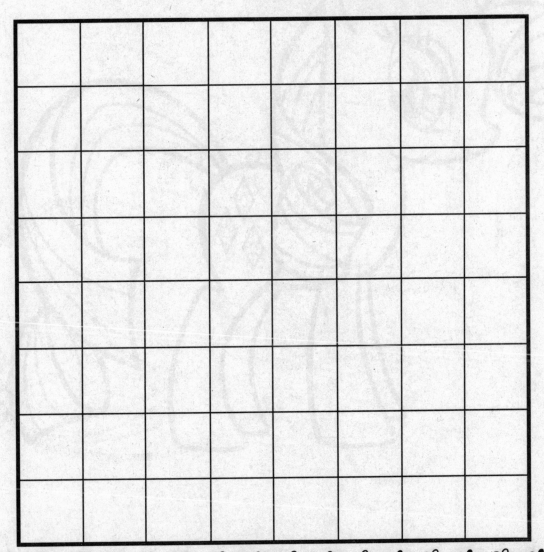

TWiN PONiES!

Can you find the two ponies that are exactly the same?

1.

2.

3.

4.

princess celestia

HOW MANY?

Count the items below and
place your answer on the line.

_____ SUNS.

Answer: 9 Suns.

SPIKE THE DRAGON

COLOR BY NUMBER

Use the key below
to color the picture.

1. blue 2. green 3. purple

PONY MAZE

Follow the path of cupcakes to help
Pinkie Pie find her way to Rainbow Dash.

pony
pals

TWIN PONIES!

Can you find the two ponies that are exactly the same?

Answer: 2 and 3 are the same.

HOW MANY?

Count the items below and place your answer on the line.

_____ BALLOONS.

MY LiTTLE PONY MiX–UP

Unscramble the words below.

URLER

_____

SNU

_____

RPiNCSSE

_____

MAKE A MATCH

Look at the 3 ponies in each column. Find the ponies that match and draw a line connecting the two.

TWiN PONiES!

Can you find the two ponies that are exactly the same?

FUN FiLL-iNS

Fill in the missing letters to reveal each word below.

HINT: Princess Celestia wants Twilight Sparkle to find the meaning of:

T _ E

MA _ iC _ F

F _ iE DS _ iP

TWILIGHT SPARKLE &
SPIKE THE DRAGON

Sweet Apple ACRES

PONY MAZE

Follow the path of apples to help
Applejack find her way to Sweet Apple Acres.

TiC-TAC-TOE

The object of Tic–Tac–Toe is to get three in a row. The first player is known as X and the second is O. Players alternate placing X's and O's on the game board until either opponent has three in a row or all nine squares are filled. X always goes first, and in the event that no one has three in a row, the tie game is called a cat's game!

EXAMPLE

INITIALS	POINTS
CAT	

FUN FiLL-iNS

Fill in the missing letters to reveal each word below.

HINT: They follow Fluttershy wherever she goes:

TRA_L _F

B_TTERF_iES

MAKE A MATCH

Look at the 3 ponies in each column. Find the ponies that match and draw a line connecting the two.

HOW MANY?

Count the items below and place your answer on the line.

_____ FLOWERS.

LET'S DRAW!

Twilight Sparkle loves to read.
Draw some books.

HOW MANY?

Count the items below and place your answer on the line.

_____ BUNNIES.

MAKE A MATCH

Look at the 3 ponies in each column. Find the ponies that match and draw a line connecting the two.

CONNECT THE DOTS

Connect the dots by alphabetical order.

HOW MANY?

Count the items below and place your answer on the line.

_____ RAINBOWS.

Answer: 6 Rainbows

Princess Celestia

TIC-TAC-TOE

The object of Tic—Tac—Toe is to get three in a row. The first player is known as X and the second is O. Players alternate placing X's and O's on the game board until either opponent has three in a row or all nine squares are filled. X always goes first, and in the event that no one has three in a row, the tie game is called a cat's game!

EXAMPLE

INITIALS	POINTS
CAT	

LET'S DRAW!

Use the grid
to help you draw
a butterfly.

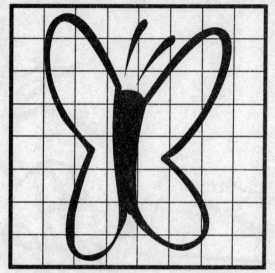

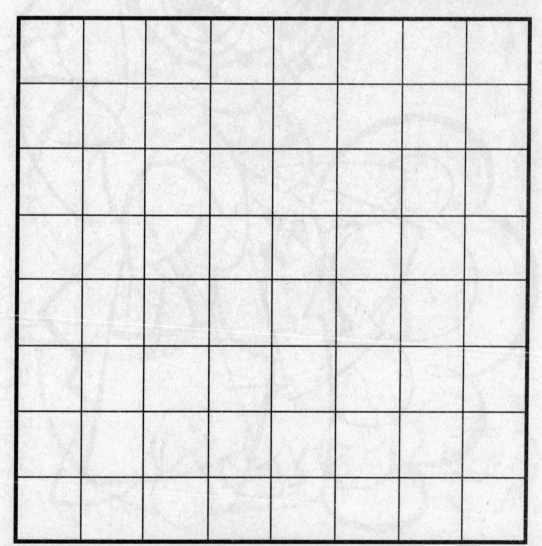

TWiN PONiES!

Can you find the two ponies that are exactly the same?

1.

2.

3.

4.

PONY MAZE

Help Rarity find her way to the gems.

start

finish

HOW MANY?

Count the items below and place your answer on the line.

_____ DIAMOND RINGS.

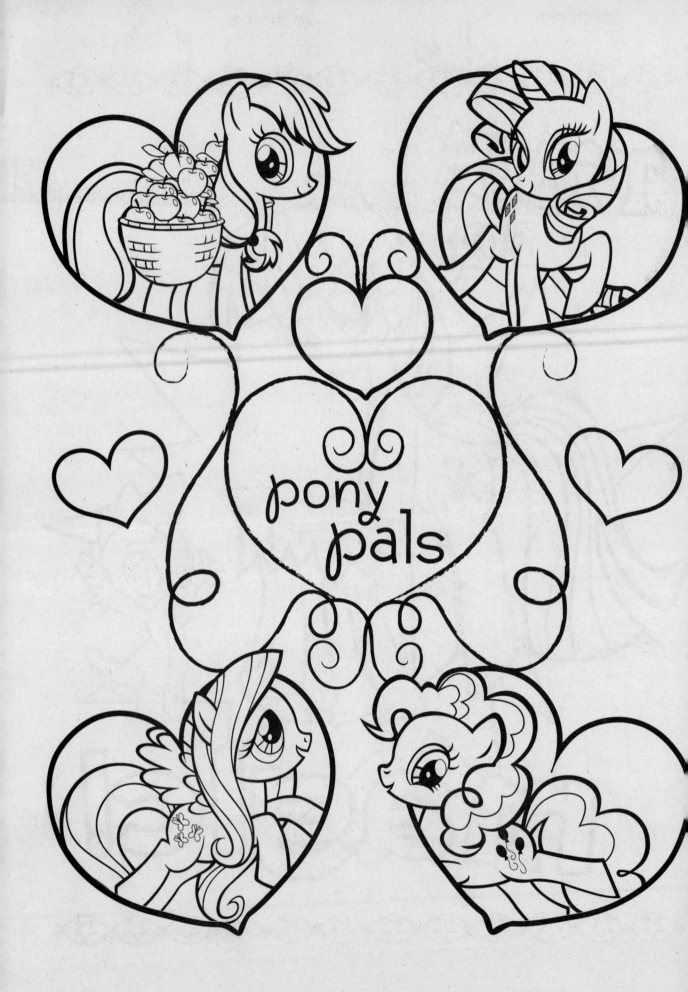